A TRUE BOOK

My United States
Washington, D.C.

KAREN KELLAHER

Children's Press®
An Imprint of Scholastic Inc.

Content Consultant

James Wolfinger, PhD, Associate Dean and Professor
College of Education, DePaul University, Chicago, Illinois

Library of Congress Cataloging-in-Publication Data
Names: Kellaher, Karen, author.
Title: Washington, D.C. / by Karen Kellaher.
Description: New York : Children's Press, an imprint of Scholastic Inc., 2018. | Series: A true book | Includes
   bibliographical references and index.
Identifiers: LCCN 2017025789 | ISBN 9780531231722 (library binding) | ISBN 9780531247235 (pbk.)
Subjects: LCSH: Washington (D.C.)—Juvenile literature.
Classification: LCC F194.3 .K45 2018 | DDC 975.3—dc23
LC record available at https://lccn.loc.gov/2017025789

Front cover: Washington Monument

Back cover: Dinosaur skeleton

Welcome to Washington, D.C.

Find the Truth!

Everything you are about to read is true *except* for one of the sentences on this page.

Which one is **TRUE**?

T or F Washington, D.C., is home to the world's biggest library.

T or F Every American president has lived and worked in Washington, D.C.

 Find the answers in this book.

Key Facts

Full Name: Washington, District of Columbia

Status: The U.S. capital is not part of any state. It is a special district run by the U.S. government.

Estimated population as of 2016: 681,170

UNITED STATES

Washington, D.C.

Contents

Map: This Is Washington, D.C.! **6**

1 Land and Wildlife

What is the terrain of Washington, D.C.,
like and what lives there? **9**

2 Government

What are the different parts of the
Washington, D.C., government? **17**

THE BIG TRUTH!

What Represents Washington, D.C.?

Which designs, objects,
plants, and animals symbolize
Washington, D.C.? **22**

American Beauty rose

Wood thrush

4

3 History

How did Washington, D.C., become
the city it is today?........................... 25

4 Culture

What do the people of Washington, D.C.,
do for work and fun? 35

Famous People 42

Did You Know That 44

Resources 46

Important Words............ 47

Index 48

About the Author........... 48

Olympian Katie Ledecky

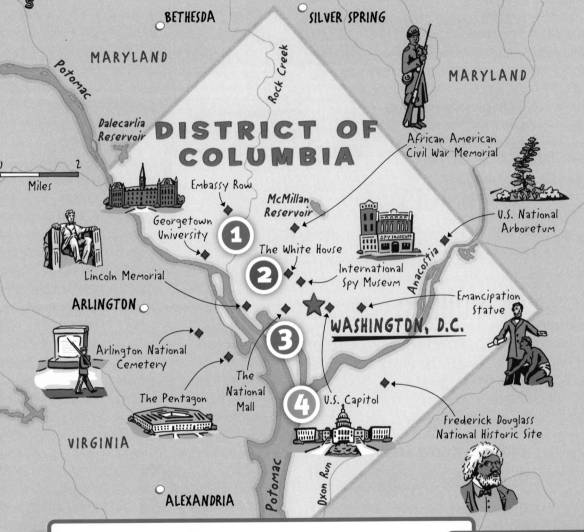

N
W E
S

BETHESDA

SILVER SPRING

MARYLAND

MARYLAND

Potomac

Rock Creek

Dalecarlia Reservoir

DISTRICT OF COLUMBIA

African American Civil War Memorial

0 2
Miles

Embassy Row

McMillan Reservoir

U.S. National Arboretum

Georgetown University

1

The White House

Lincoln Memorial

2

International Spy Museum

SPY MUSEUM

Anacostia

Emancipation Statue

ARLINGTON

3

WASHINGTON, D.C.

Arlington National Cemetery

The National Mall

U.S. Capitol

The Pentagon

4

Frederick Douglass National Historic Site

VIRGINIA

Potomac

Oxon Run

ALEXANDRIA

1 Embassy Row

Countries around the globe send representatives called ambassadors to the United States. Many ambassadors live and work in a section of Washington, D.C., called Embassy Row. They fly the flags of their home countries outside their buildings.

② The White House

The mansion where the president lives and works has six floors, 132 rooms, and 35 bathrooms. It even has its own movie theater (pictured here) and bowling alley. Visitors can tour some parts of the building.

③ The National Mall

This mall is not for shopping! It's a 2-mile-long (3-kilometer) grassy area lined with monuments, memorials, and museums. One of the most famous examples is the beautiful Lincoln Memorial, built to honor Abraham Lincoln, the country's 16th president.

④ U.S. Capitol

Don't let the spelling confuse you! The word *capital* (with an *a*) refers to the whole city of Washington, D.C. But the Capitol (with an *o*) is the building where members of Congress meet to make the country's laws. It sits on a small hill known as Capitol Hill.

Nearly one-fifth of the land in Washington, D.C., is protected as parkland.

CHAPTER 1

Land and Wildlife

Washington, D.C., is nestled on the eastern bank of the Potomac River between the states of Maryland and Virginia. It covers an area of about 68 square miles (176 square kilometers). Hundreds of years ago, the area where Washington, D.C., now sits was mostly covered with forests and marshes. Today, it is a bustling **urban** area and the center of our nation's government. But this busy city still has plenty of nature for residents and visitors to enjoy.

Lay of the Land

Most of Washington, D.C., is part of a **geological** region called the Atlantic Coastal Plain. The land there is mostly flat and low. The city's northwest corner is part of a region called the Piedmont Plateau. It is known for its rolling hills. The lowest point in the city is the Potomac River, which is at sea level. The highest point is Point Reno in the northwest section. It is 409 feet (125 meters) above sea level.

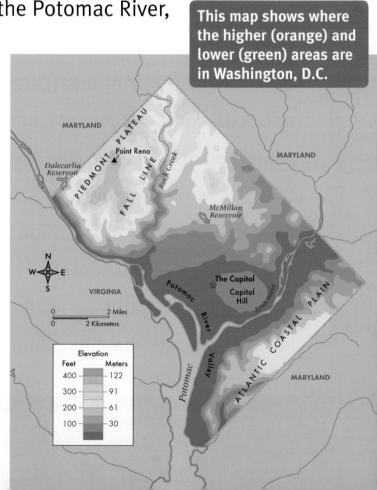

This map shows where the higher (orange) and lower (green) areas are in Washington, D.C.

MARYLAND

PIEDMONT PLATEAU

Point Reno

FALL LINE

Dalecarlia Reservoir

Rock Creek

MARYLAND

McMillan Reservoir

N
W · E
S

VIRGINIA

Potomac

The Capitol
Capitol Hill

Anacostia

0   2 Miles
0   2 Kilometers

Potomac River

Valley

ATLANTIC COASTAL PLAIN

MARYLAND

Elevation
Feet	Meters
400	122
300	91
200	61
100	30

The Francis Scott Key Bridge spans the Potomac River, connecting Washington, D.C., to Arlington, Virginia.

Two Rivers

Washington, D.C., has two rivers that come together to form a Y shape. The Potomac River flows southeast along the city's western border. The Anacostia River flows southwest across the city and joins the Potomac. There are several tiny islands within both rivers.

Other bodies of water in the capital include creeks and streams. The Tidal Basin is a special pool that was dug alongside the Potomac. It helps keep the river from overflowing into the city.

Climate

Residents of Washington, D.C., need to be ready for all kinds of weather. Rain falls about once every three days. Summers can get hot and sticky, with temperatures rising above 85 degrees Fahrenheit (29 degrees Celsius). Cooler temperatures make spring and fall popular times for tourists to visit the nation's capital. Washington's winters tend to be fairly mild. The city usually gets no more than 15 inches (38 centimeters) of snow a year. But once every few years, big winter storms bring 3 feet (1 m) of snow or more!

MAXIMUM TEMPERATURE
106°F

MINIMUM TEMPERATURE
15°F

A little girl dances in the rain in front of the White House on the Fourth of July.

When most people think of Washington, D.C., they probably don't picture a leafy wilderness. But the capital is home to one of the biggest city parks in the United States. Rock Creek Park in the northwestern part of the city covers more than 1,700 **acres** (688 hectares). This makes it twice the size of New York City's famous Central Park. Congress created the park in 1890 to preserve a piece of the city's natural environment. Visitors can hike along forest trails, go canoeing in Rock Creek, look for wildlife, and more.

Cyclists enjoy the bike path at Rock Creek Park.

A Peek at Plants

Washington, D.C., is known for its Japanese cherry trees, which produce beautiful pink and white blossoms every spring. But these trees did not always grow in the city. The original cherry trees were a gift from the mayor of Tokyo, Japan, in 1912.

Many **native** plants also grow in America's capital. Oaks, lindens, and elms line many city streets. These and other tree species fill the capital's parks. Wildflowers such as violets, bluebells, and bloodroots add a splash of color to the parks in the spring and summer.

Cherry blossoms create some of Washington's most beautiful scenery.

Hay's Spring amphipods are less than 1 inch (2.5 cm) long.

Capital Creatures

Many animals make their home in Washington, D.C. Mammals such as white-tailed deer, gray squirrels, rabbits, raccoons, and bats called flying foxes live in the city's wooded parks. Experts have spotted dozens of species of birds there, from colorful cardinals to majestic bald eagles.

The city's rivers and creeks are habitats for many species of fish, including carp, bass, and perch. Rock Creek is home to the Hay's Spring amphipod, a tiny, see-through creature that looks like a shrimp. This endangered species lives nowhere else in the world.

The dome of the U.S. Capitol has 108 windows.

CHAPTER 2

Government

Most cities and towns in the United States operate under three layers of government—a local or city government, a state government, and the U.S. **federal** government. But Washington, D.C., is a little different. It is not a state, so it has no governor or state lawmaking body. As the nation's capital, it is overseen directly by the federal government. There is a city government, but its power is limited.

President George W. Bush speaks before all 535 members of Congress in 2005.

Three Branches

Washington, D.C., is the seat of the U.S. federal government. The president of the United States heads the **executive** branch. Congress, the **legislative** branch of the government, meets in the U.S. Capitol. Congress has two parts: the Senate and the House of Representatives. Its members write our nation's laws. The U.S. Supreme Court decides the nation's most important legal cases. It leads the **judicial** branch.

Who's in Charge?

At one time, the federal government had complete authority over Washington, D.C. But in 1973, Congress gave home rule to the people of the city, allowing them to create a local government. Today, voters in Washington, D.C., elect a mayor and a city council with 13 members. The city government makes decisions about the city's schools, street repairs, and other local issues. But the federal government still plays a big role. Every law that Washington's city government passes must be approved by the U.S. Congress.

DISTRICT GOVERNMENT

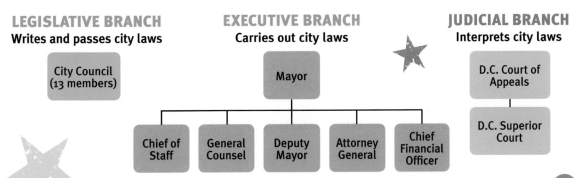

LEGISLATIVE BRANCH
Writes and passes city laws

- City Council (13 members)

EXECUTIVE BRANCH
Carries out city laws

- Mayor
  - Chief of Staff
  - General Counsel
  - Deputy Mayor
  - Attorney General
  - Chief Financial Officer

JUDICIAL BRANCH
Interprets city laws

- D.C. Court of Appeals
- D.C. Superior Court

19

Having a Say

People in Washington, D.C., have a limited voice in the U.S. Congress. They do not elect any of the country's 100 senators. They send one **delegate** to the House of Representatives, but he or she is not allowed to vote on laws. Many D.C. residents argue that this system is unfair. Some want their city to become a state so they can have representation in Congress.

Residents have a bigger say when it comes to the U.S. executive branch. The district has three electoral votes in presidential elections. This wasn't always the case. Until 1961, D.C. didn't get any electoral votes at all. However, the 23rd Amendment to the U.S. Constitution granted D.C. a number of electoral votes equal to the least populous state in the country.

Representing Washington, D.C.

Elected officials in Washington, D.C. represent a population with a range of interests, lifestyles, and backgrounds.

Ethnicity (2016 estimates)

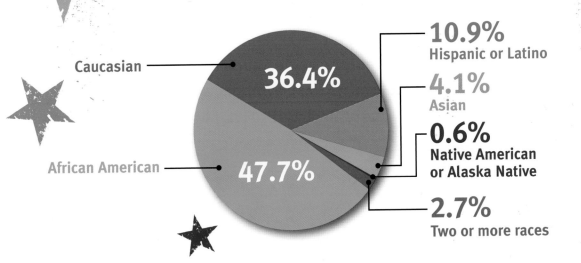

Caucasian — 36.4%

African American — 47.7%

10.9% Hispanic or Latino

4.1% Asian

0.6% Native American or Alaska Native

2.7% Two or more races

17% speak a language other than English at home.

18% are kids under age 18.

41% own their homes.

89% of the population graduated from high school.

55% of the population have a degree beyond high school.

14% of Washingtonians were born in other countries.

What Represents Washington, D.C.?

Like the 50 states, Washington, D.C., chooses specific animals, plants, and objects to represent the values and characteristics of its land and its people. Find out why these symbols were chosen to represent Washington, D.C., or discover surprising curiosities about them.

Seal

The woman in the long robe represents justice, and the statue is of George Washington, America's first president. In the background are the Potomac River and the U.S. Capitol.

Flag

The Washington, D.C., flag is based on a crest, or symbol, once used by George Washington's family. Washington chose the site for the capital city.

American Beauty Rose

OFFICIAL FLOWER

Although it has not been proven, some people believe this rose was first grown in the White House garden.

Potomac Bluestone

OFFICIAL ROCK

This stone was used to build parts of the White House and the U.S. Capitol.

Scarlet Oak

OFFICIAL TREE

The scarlet oak's leaves are green most of the year, but they turn deep red each fall.

Capitalsaurus

OFFICIAL DINOSAUR

In 1898, part of the backbone of a dinosaur was unearthed in Washington, D.C. Nearly 100 years later, a scientist studied the fossil and nicknamed the dinosaur Capitalsaurus.

Wood Thrush

OFFICIAL BIRD

This small songbird lives in D.C. during spring and summer and flies south during colder months.

The original White House took eight years to build and cost $232,372.

CHAPTER 3

History

Washington, D.C., is named for George Washington, America's first president. But surprisingly, he never lived there! In 1790, the country was ready to build its permanent capital. Washington chose the location and hired experts to plan the city. But by the time the city was ready, Washington was no longer in office. President John Adams and about 125 other government employees moved to Washington, D.C., in 1800. It was an important chapter in the district's long and busy history.

Early History

People have been living in the area that is now Washington, D.C., for at least 12,000 years. The region's earliest residents fished in the Potomac River, hunted deer and other animals, and gathered wild nuts and berries.

Over time, the main Native American group in the region became known as the Piscataway. They made homes by bending young trees into arches and covering the arches with mats made of woven grass. Like their early **ancestors**, they fished and hunted. They also grew corn, squash, and beans.

This map shows where the Piscataway lived in what is now Washington, D.C., before Europeans came.

In the 1600s, the first Europeans arrived in the area. In 1608, Captain John Smith sailed up the Potomac from an English **settlement** in Jamestown, Virginia. He visited a Piscataway village before returning to

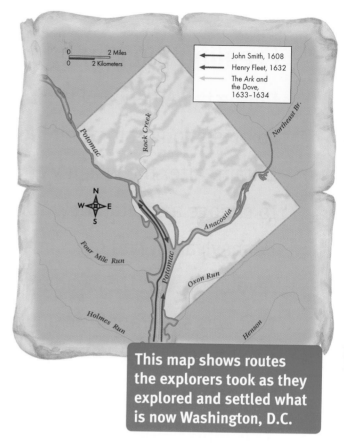

This map shows routes the explorers took as they explored and settled what is now Washington, D.C.

Jamestown. Other Europeans soon followed and settled in the area. Before long, many Piscataway fell sick with diseases such as measles and smallpox, which the newcomers had carried from Europe. Entire villages were wiped out. By 1700, most of the surviving Piscataway had moved out of the area.

Creating the Capital

During the American Revolution (1775–1783), colonists fought for their independence from Great Britain. After the war, it was time for the new nation to choose a capital. New York City and Philadelphia, Pennsylvania, had been important cities during the revolution, but U.S. leaders wanted a capital city that was separate from any state. In 1790, George Washington selected a diamond-shaped area along the Potomac River to be the site for the capital. This land belonged to Virginia and Maryland, which donated it to the U.S. government.

At Independence Hall in Philadelphia, Pennsylvania, the country's Founding Fathers gathered during the revolution to create the Declaration of Independence and the U.S. Constitution.

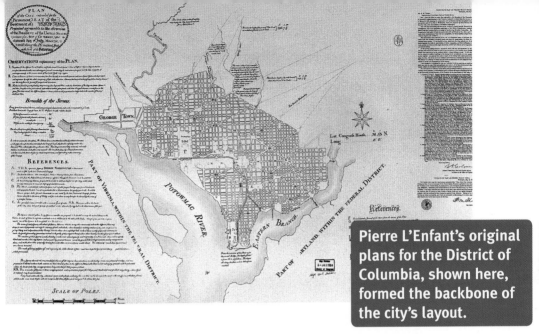

Pierre L'Enfant's original plans for the District of Columbia, shown here, formed the backbone of the city's layout.

To design the city, Washington hired a French engineer named Pierre L'Enfant. L'Enfant made grand plans. He imagined a capitol built on a hill with wide avenues stretching out from it. He planned spaces for monuments and fountains. But L'Enfant argued with local landowners and was soon fired. Washington hired a new surveyor named Andrew Ellicott to finish the plans. By 1793, construction was under way. Hundreds of workers, including many slaves, built the Capitol, the White House, and other buildings.

A Rough Start

Much of the capital was still under construction when tragedy struck. In 1812, the United States and Great Britain went to war because of conflicts their ships were having at sea. In August 1814, British troops attacked Washington, D.C. They set fire to the Capitol, the White House, and other public buildings. It took years to rebuild.

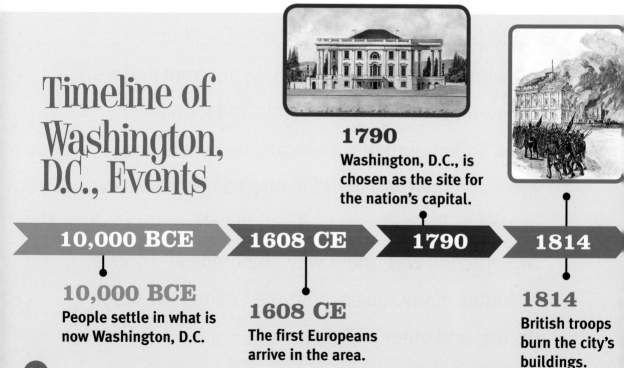

Timeline of Washington, D.C., Events

1790
Washington, D.C., is chosen as the site for the nation's capital.

| 10,000 BCE | 1608 CE | 1790 | 1814 |

10,000 BCE
People settle in what is now Washington, D.C.

1608 CE
The first Europeans arrive in the area.

1814
British troops burn the city's buildings.

Time of Change

From 1861 to 1865, Washington, D.C., felt the strain of the Civil War. The city was the capital of the Union, but it bordered the Confederate state of Virginia. Thousands of Union soldiers were stationed in Washington to protect the capital. After the war, many freed slaves made their homes in the city. The city's population grew quickly.

1865
Abraham Lincoln is shot and killed in Washington, D.C.'s Ford's Theater—the first U.S. president to be assassinated.

2017
About half a million women participate in the Women's March, one of the largest protests in the capital's history.

| 1848 | 1865 | 2001 | 2017 |

1848
Work begins on the Washington Monument, a monument to the country's first president; it wasn't completed until 1884.

2001
Security in the capital is permanently increased after terrorists attack the United States.

Martin Luther King Jr. waves to the crowd from the steps of the Lincoln Memorial.

In the 1900s, Washington, D.C., began to look more like the grand city that Pierre L'Enfant had once envisioned. The National Mall was created, and many monuments were built.

In the 1960s, the capital became an important location in the civil rights movement. In 1963, Dr. Martin Luther King Jr. gave his famous "I Have a Dream" speech on the steps of the Lincoln Memorial. Today, the capital is still a place where people go to express their views and their hopes for the country's future.

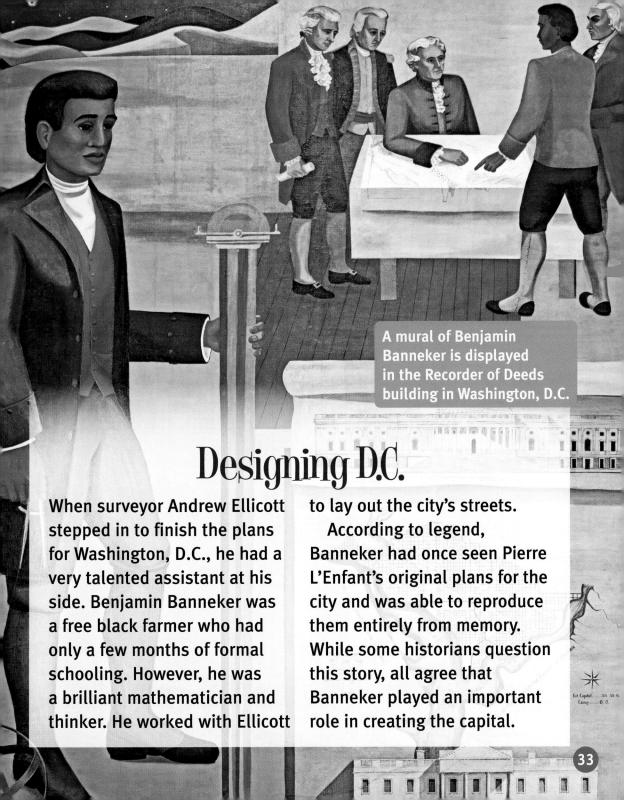

A mural of Benjamin Banneker is displayed in the Recorder of Deeds building in Washington, D.C.

Designing D.C.

When surveyor Andrew Ellicott stepped in to finish the plans for Washington, D.C., he had a very talented assistant at his side. Benjamin Banneker was a free black farmer who had only a few months of formal schooling. However, he was a brilliant mathematician and thinker. He worked with Ellicott to lay out the city's streets.

According to legend, Banneker had once seen Pierre L'Enfant's original plans for the city and was able to reproduce them entirely from memory. While some historians question this story, all agree that Banneker played an important role in creating the capital.

The Library of Congress has more than 38 million books and other printed materials.

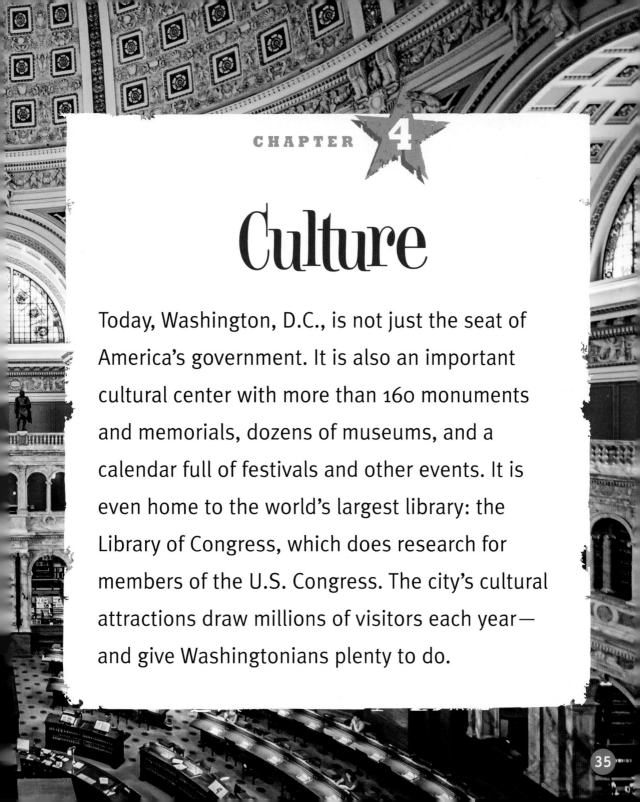

CHAPTER 4

Culture

Today, Washington, D.C., is not just the seat of America's government. It is also an important cultural center with more than 160 monuments and memorials, dozens of museums, and a calendar full of festivals and other events. It is even home to the world's largest library: the Library of Congress, which does research for members of the U.S. Congress. The city's cultural attractions draw millions of visitors each year— and give Washingtonians plenty to do.

Many historic airplanes are on display at the National Air and Space Museum of the Smithsonian Institution.

Monuments and Museums

Monuments and memorials have been built in the capital to remember people and events in U.S. history. Some honor presidents and other leaders, such as Martin Luther King Jr. Others, such as the Vietnam Veterans Memorial, pay **tribute** to people who fought in wars.

The city's museums offer something for everyone. Nineteen of them make up a group of museums called the Smithsonian Institution.

Festival Time

There's often something special to celebrate in the nation's capital. Every spring when the cherry trees bloom, people head downtown for the three-week-long Cherry Blossom Festival. They enjoy concerts, fireworks, and kite-flying contests. On April 16 each year, Washingtonians celebrate Emancipation Day. This holiday recalls the day in 1862 when slaves in the capital city were freed. Public schools close for the day, and marching bands parade through the city.

A marching band parades in front of the National Archives Building during the National Cherry Blossom Festival.

Sports and Recreation

Washingtonians have plenty of recreation options to choose from. They can walk, run, or bike on the city's many park trails or play with their pets in a dozen dog parks.

Residents can also watch professional sports teams play. The Nationals baseball team, the Wizards and Mystics basketball teams, the Redskins football team, the Capitals hockey team, and the D.C. United soccer team all call Washington, D.C., home.

The Washington Mystics basketball team has been wowing fans since 1998.

Many workers in Washington, D.C., rely on the city's subway system, the Metro, to get to their jobs each day.

At Work in the Capital

Government is the biggest employer in Washington, D.C. About four out of every 10 employed adults in the city work for the federal government or the local city government. Many other people in the capital have jobs related to tourism. They work in hotels, restaurants, museums, and other places that tourists visit.

Many young people head to Washington, D.C., to prepare for future careers. The city has seven major colleges and universities and several smaller ones.

On the Menu

Cuisine in the capital is diverse. Because the city is not far from the Atlantic Ocean, crabs, fish, and other kinds of seafood are among the favorite dishes. Southern specialties like fried chicken and grits are also popular. And over time, immigrants from around the world have brought international flavors to D.C.'s markets and menus.

  ## Senate Bean Soup

Ask an adult to help you!

No food says Washington, D.C., like Senate Bean Soup. It has been served in the dining room of the U.S. Senate every day for more than 100 years!

Ingredients

2 pounds dried navy beans
4 quarts hot water
1 1/2 pounds smoked ham hocks

1 onion, chopped
2 tablespoons butter
Salt and pepper

Directions

Rinse the beans under hot water. Place the beans, hot water, and ham hocks in a large pot. Cover the pot and put it on the stovetop. Simmer on low heat for 3 hours, stirring once in a while. Carefully remove the ham hocks. Dice the meat and put it back into the pot. Brown the onion in the butter, then add it to the soup. Bring to a boil, then turn off the heat. Add a bit of salt and pepper to taste. Enjoy!

A Spectacular City

Washington, D.C., may not be large in area, but it is big on history and culture. As the seat of America's federal government, it also plays a very important role in the nation. The people who live and work in Washington, D.C., know how special the capital city is. And every year, millions of visitors discover the district's magic for themselves. ★

The Washington Monument is visible from many parts of Washington, D.C.

Famous People

John Philip Sousa

(1854–1932) wrote many of the patriotic songs that Americans march to in parades. One of his most famous songs is "The Stars and Stripes Forever," the official march song of the United States.

Benjamin O. Davis Sr.

(1877–1970) was the U.S. Army's first African American general. He fought in several wars and helped end racial discrimination in the Army.

J. Edgar Hoover

(1895–1972) was in charge of the Federal Bureau of Investigation (FBI) for many decades. Today, the FBI building is named for him.

Marjorie Kinnan Rawlings

(1896–1953) was a famous author. She wrote *The Yearling*, a book about a boy and his pet deer.

Duke Ellington

(1899–1974) was a great jazz musician who was born Edward Kennedy Ellington. He wrote more than 3,000 songs, played the piano, and led an award-winning orchestra.

Evelyn Boyd Granville

(1924–) is a retired mathematician. She worked on computer software that helped the U.S. send the first American into space in 1961.

Connie Chung

(1946–) is a well-known TV journalist. In 1993, she became the first Asian American—and only the second woman—to work as a news anchor on a major American TV network.

Samuel L. Jackson

(1948–) is one of the highest paid actors of all time. You might know him as a Jedi Master in some of the *Star Wars* films.

Al Gore

(1948–) served as vice president of the United States from 1993 to 2001.

Bill Nye

(1955–) is a scientist and TV personality. He hosted a popular show for kids called *Bill Nye the Science Guy*. He has also written several science books.

Katie Ledecky

(1997–) is one of America's fastest female swimmers. By the time she turned 20, she had won five Olympic gold medals and shattered 13 world records.

Did You Know That ...

Washington, D.C., has a museum that's all about spies and spying.

Members of the U.S. Congress have a private subway system to take them from the Capitol to their offices.

You can see the real Declaration of Independence and U.S. Constitution in the capital's National Archives.

The White House wasn't called the White House until 1901. Before that, it was known as the President's House or the President's Palace.

Tens of thousands of people work in Washington, D.C., but live in nearby towns in Virginia and Maryland. They drive cars or take trains or buses into the capital.

Some unusual pets have lived in the White House. Presidents John Quincy Adams and Herbert Hoover both had pet alligators. Abraham Lincoln's family had two goats. And Teddy Roosevelt's kids had a pig, a pony, a snake, and even a one-legged rooster!

The top of the Washington Monument is a slightly different color from the bottom. Builders used stone from two different places.

The Smithsonian's National Zoo has more than 1,500 animals. Zoo biologists work to increase populations of endangered animals.

Did you find the truth?

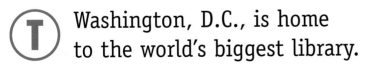

 T Washington, D.C., is home to the world's biggest library.

F Every American president has lived and worked in Washington, D.C.

Resources

Books

Nonfiction

Falk, Laine. *What's in Washington, D.C.?* New York: Children's Press, 2009.

Hill, Isabel. *Urban Animals of Washington, D.C.* Cambridge, MA: Star Bright Books, 2013.

Kent, Deborah. *Washington, D.C.* New York: Children's Press, 2010.

Fiction

Blume, Judy. *Double Fudge.* New York: Dutton Children's Books, 2002.

Cabot, Meg. *All-American Girl.* New York: HarperCollins, 2002.

Visit this Scholastic website for more information on Washington, D.C.:

★ www.factsfornow.scholastic.com
Enter the keywords **Washington, D.C.**

Important Words

acres (AY-kurz) a measurement of area; one acre is equal to 43,560 square feet

ancestors (AN-ses-turz) members of one's family who lived long ago

delegate (DEL-uh-guht) someone who represents other people at a meeting

executive (eg-ZEK-yuh-tiv) belonging to the branch of government that executes or carries out laws

federal (FED-ur-uhl) having to do with the national government, as opposed to state or local governments

geological (jee-uh-LAH-jih-kuhl) having to do with earth's layers of soil and rock

judicial (joo-DISH-uhl) belonging to the branch of government that includes courts of law

legislative (LEJ-uh-slay-tiv) belonging to the branch of government that makes laws

native (NAY-tiv) belonging in or originating in a certain place

settlement (SET-uhl-muhnt) a small village; a group of people who have left one place to make a home in another

tribute (TRIB-yoot) something done, given, or said to show thanks or respect

urban (UR-buhn) having to do with a city

Index

Page numbers in **bold** indicate illustrations.

Adams, John, 25
American Revolution, 28
amphipods, **15**
Anacostia River, 11
animals, 15, **23**, 26, **45**

Banneker, Benjamin, 33
birds, 15, **23**

cherry trees, **14**, **37**
city government, 17, 19, 39
civil rights movement, **32**
Civil War, 31
climate, **12**

dinosaurs, **23**
diseases, 27

education, 19, 21, 37, 39
elections, 19, 20
elevation, **10**
Ellicott, Andrew, 29, 33
Embassy Row, 6
explorers, **27**, 28

famous people, **42–43**
festivals, **37**
fish, 15, 26, 40
food, 26, **40**

jobs, 39, **44**

King, Martin Luther, Jr., **32**, 36

land, **8–9**, **10**
languages, 21
L'Enfant, Pierre, 29, 32, 33
Library of Congress, **34–35**
Lincoln, Abraham, 7, **31**, 45
Lincoln Memorial, **7**, 32
location, 25, 28

maps, **6–7**, **10**, **26**, **28**
memorials, **7**, 32, 35, 36
monuments, 7, 29, **31**, 32, 35, 36, **45**
museums, 7, 35, **36**, 39, 44
music, **42**

national government, 7, **16–17**, 18, **19**, 20, **24–25**, 28, **29**, **30**, **31**, 39, **42**, **43**, **44**
National Mall, **7**, **32**
Native Americans, 21, 26, **27**

planning, 25, 29, **33**
plants, **14**, **23**, 26
Potomac River, 9, 10, **11**, **22**, 26, 27, 28

recipe, **40**
Rock Creek Park, **13**, 15

settlers, 27, **28**, 30
slavery, 29, 31, 37
Smith, John, **27**
Smithsonian Institution, **36**, 45
sports, **38**, **43**
symbols, **22–23**

terrorism, **31**
timeline, **30–31**
tourism, 12, 39

U.S. Capitol, **7**, **16–17**, 18, **22**, 23, 29, 30, 44
U.S. Congress, 13, 18, **19**, 20, 35, 44

War of 1812, **30**
Washington, George, 22, 25, 28, 29
Washington Monument, **31**, **41**, **45**
White House, **7**, 23, **24–25**, 29, 30, **44**, 45
wildflowers, 14, **23**
Women's March, **31**

About the Author

Karen Kellaher is an editor in Scholastic's classroom magazine division and has written more than 20 books for kids and teachers. She holds a bachelor's degree in communications from the University of Scranton (Pennsylvania) and a master's degree combining elementary education and publishing from New York University's Gallatin School of Individualized Study.